Emotions in Motion

Shantell Jefferson

PublishAmerica
Baltimore

© 2006 by Shantell Jefferson.
All rights reserved. No part of this book may be reproduced, stored in a retrieval system or transmitted in any form or by any means without the prior written permission of the publishers, except by a reviewer who may quote brief passages in a review to be printed in a newspaper, magazine or journal.

First printing

At the specific preference of the author, PublishAmerica allowed this work to remain exactly as the author intended, verbatim, without editorial input.

ISBN: 1-4241-5873-7
PUBLISHED BY PUBLISHAMERICA, LLLP
www.publishamerica.com
Baltimore

Printed in the United States of America

Dedication

I would like to dedicate this book to the most influential people in my life. First my heavenly father God for being my source from which all my love, help, and gifts come from. The faith of a mustard seed does truly move mountains. Thank you for moving in me. Secondly to my mother, Clara who I thought never loved me enough to like me. Oh how God showed us we were both so wrong about each other. He restored that mother daughter bond that can't be substituted. I love you so very much. I am so glad we didn't have to lose one another before we both realized how very much we needed each other. Next to my father Eddie who called me red rover his faithful and loyal companion. He read to me daily giving me the desires to want to do the same. We have weathered the storm and no matter what you did wrong you always told me do right it will come back bearing good fruits. Finally, to my daughters Nastavyia and Nadyia for giving me love unconditionally. Being a beacon of light to keep me from driving off this sometimes miserable road called life and trying to end it all. Thank you for your forgiveness and compassion toward me even when I didn't deserve it because I was to blinded by my own destruction I couldn't see through the fog enough to rescue you girls fast enough from the very hell I was trying so desperately to protect you from. Mommy loves you both so very much. I thank Jesus for interceding to the father on our behalf making us over a brand new family again shining bright in his light.

Acknowledgments

I would like to acknowledge God with him all things are possible. Mother thank you for introducing me to PublishAmerica and pushing me to submit my work to there company. My father for believing this could be more than a dream. To my loyal sisters Kimberly, Leola and Nikia, to the shield and protector my brother Eddie the 2nd, to my guardian angels Nastavyia and Nadyia, The way of the world was unjust to us all causing hurt and pain but it never changed our love for one another. To mama haze (Hazel Young) and Eliza Horton for listening to my poems at all hours of the day and night. Thank you both for being my #1 fan. To Susan Noland and the Dress for Success Organization for giving me a hand up and allowing me to use our PWG meetings as a forum to read my works to a fabulous group of women's all striving to succeed in life despite the struggles that come there way. Dewanna Lovelace for being my friend and not seeing me as just another case # to be worked, I love you more than you'll ever know. My best friend Judy Perez for always seeing the real me despite my circumstances, your more than my friend you are my sister in in arms. I love you. Last but not least to Charles Tanner, Chelette Davis, Faye Wilson and Carolyn Tillis for you're right on time blessings from the Lord.

Table of Contents

Chapter 1
All About Me *happy and sad, loved and hated*................ 11

Chapter 2
Matters of the Heart *love romance and relationships* 25

Chapter 3
Mother and Child *a family too* 49

Chapter 4
Deliverance *Christianity, inspirational, prayer* 59

*Emotions
in Motion*

Chapter 1

All About Me
happy and sad, loved and hated

Beauty
Here in This Box
To Be Whole
Happy Birthday
Loves Deception
Stage Fright
Love Is
Black Sheep
Love Is a Four-Letter Word
Ghost Memory Quilt

Beauty

Beauty is only skin deep. Yet we plant a seed, grow it, protect it, and covet it. As if it were a child needing to be cared for and taught.
Beauty is only skin deep.
Yet people will make up themselves, cut themselves and inject themselves all in the name of projecting beauty.
They will shed themselves, become someone or something else for beauty, but it is only skin deep.
Deep is how far they go never knowing that they have lost sight on what real beauty is.
Beauty is bring a new child in the world. Beauty is the dew dripping off a flower at sunrise.
Beauty is the mating of two birds in mid flight in the sky. Beauty is the sparkle showing in your eye, that gleam in your smile.
Even the most ugliest thing on earth possess beauty because it's beauty comes from the inside out.

Here in This Box

Here in this box are many memories.
Some good, some bad, some happy, and some sad memories lay in this box.
Here in this box are pictures that bring back a flood of emotions.
Here in this box are letters that bring back flashes of friends.
Here in this box are tattering of cloth that bring back smells of places long gone.
Here in this box are thing that make life touchable.
Here in this box the memories never fade because they are safely packed away in my soul and vaulted in my mind.
Here in this box it never gets full.
In fact it always eager to receive something new here in this box.

To Be Whole

To be whole you must be strong.
You must admit when you are wrong.
Accept your faults for what they are.
Realize what's attractive on the outside won't last.
So hopefully you used your inner beauty and were nice because when your old no one wants to care for you when they know you were mean and grumpy.
To be whole you must be spiritual.
You must praise and worship God.
You must study and desire to teach and dwell with others to prosper in his way.
To be whole you need to mix the bitter with the sweet.
See that the grass is not always greener on the other side.
Know that things are not always what they seem.
When the sun is shining on one side it may be raining down on the other.
To be whole you must be able to express emotions.
Show signs of empathy.
Be able to give with out thought of a return.
To be whole you must be able to not anger your fellow man, be no ones fool, love with out prejudice.
To be whole you must be true to yourself first and put all peer pressures to the way side.
To be whole you need to realize when your grown you can't become a child again, no matter how hard you try.
That when its gone or over it really is so. And once you lose it you cant get it back.

Happy Birthday

Happy Birthday to you, Know that today is a special day for you.
It is the day of celebration for your birth.
It marks your time and gives you something to look back on.
It too allows you to reflect on the good times during past years.
It is also your marker for coming of a new age.
A chance to dream and do all new things for another year.
To grow into your own self some more.
It is your day to shine in all your glory and splendor in the Lord.
Knowing that he loves you always and know that I too, love you!
God blessed this day especially for you.
So enjoy it from your near and dear Friend!

Love's Deception

Love is walking up the path to your front door, but beware of its knock.
It sounds so inviting, but when you let it in it surprises you.
With its sudden changes that are subtle at first glance.
But it builds up momentum like a charging bull.
Gathering speed before he runs you down. Love says do this for me, do that for me.
If you love me you'll tell me the truth.
But when you tell love the truth it slaps you hard in the face.
Snatches your heart right out your chest.
When you apologize, even when you've done no wrong.
Love harden itself against you.
Leaving you alone.
Only to catch glimpses of it now and again.
Hoping you'll beg it back in.
You will show love it has no place here anymore.
You'll close the window of opportunity up.
You'll lock the door and throw away the key.
Hell for safe measures you'll even board the damn thing up barring love out for evermore, or at least till it learns to behave its self.

Stage Fright

Do's and don't. yes and no's. the known and unknown.
Compliances and complaints. Easy and hard. You lose, you win.
Back and forth these are our struggles our battles our minds go through daily.
We move seamlessly on the outside yet inside signals have to be sent out to set ourselves in motion. It seams to all work flawlessly.
Every once in awhile ciaos breaks out. Confusion sets in and we are at a loss. We can't seem to figure right from wrong. Or which way to go or how to turn. You lay there numb to your surroundings thinking, wondering is this really real.
You close your eyes hoping when you open them something will be different. The path will be clear, you will have figured a way out.
All of a sudden you calm down. That moment of uncertainty becomes so clear. You breath deep letting out your nervous energy slowly.
You look yourself over once. You put on your best smile and you step out in front of the world.
You perform your best act yet. Being you!
The person hanging among friends, co-workers, the mommies, the daddies. The sister or brother. The next door neighbor, etc. etc.
only to have that day end back at home alone to analyze did I do it right, what could I have done differently?
You drift off to sleep with all of this on your mind only to unconsciously rise with this on your mind again to start a whole new day.
What drama will unfold on your stage today?

Love Is

Love is so fun when all is going good and everyone is happy.
But let the least bit of doubt in and then false witness begins to weaken love.
Love it self begins to be in the middle of a tug a war between two heart causing them to squeeze and press themselves against one another. One ill gotten fate and then love is no longer shared or given freely.
It becomes guarded and is stolen piece by piece. Hardening ones love from another.
Casting shadows of doubt on ones feelings about love.
It swiftly dries up and leaves like a deserted well that one provide water to a village.
Love imprison you for a life sentence.
It gives you no judge or jury to hear your case.
It says don't pass go! Don't collect $200.00.
Go straight to jail and it throws away the key.
Love is power and with out it you are only half full.
With it knowledge to control and wield it you are hopeless.
Condemn to servitude unto it. Good or bad love is a keeper it knows not how to back away.
Instead it hits you head on leaving you to fight for your own survival.
Believe me ,it does not care if you prevail or not.
Even in the end it always wins because even in death love is standing all around you.

Black Sheep! Black Sheep!

Black sheep, Black sheep with the sad brown eyes why do you cry again tonight?
Who has put the flower on your head to make you pleasing to look upon but for tells your arrival by placing a bell around your neck for all to hear so they back away from you casting more and more shame upon your head, instead of a kind word of hello.
You feel the pain from the slap on your face as yet another door is closed on your tail.
Black sheep, Black sheep what have you done to deserve such treatment? Why are you all alone and down trotting ? Where is love and kindness you so desperately seek? Why does it play hide and seek with you little black sheep?
Black sheep was a fool for love, now it has learned that love, loves nobody but love itself.
Black she prays for rain to hide its tear brought on by sorrow and pain from the people Black sheep has lost. Black sheep knows it no use to stay sad, but it can't help itself.
So, Black sheep wears a small flower to show it has a small glimmer of hope that one day by setting all it loved a drift that if it was meant to be it will come back soon.
But, if it doesn't it hopes that our father will ease the sadness away with time so that even though I may be that black sheep my brown eyes will be sad no more.

Love Is a Four-Letter Word

Love is nothing but four little letters, so you might say.
But I say love is damming and compelling.
Love will make you lose your mind and sell your soul.
Love will make you happy and sad all in the same line.
Love is all right and good.
Sometimes it even down right murderous.
Those four little letter are like dynamite waiting to deliver a powerful blow.
It doesn't care where it starts. 'Cause it's going to take you with a big bang.
It woes and coos at you seducing you right before the lights go out and the stars start spinning round about your head and that bird in the middle whistle a tune.
It can make or break a big man heart.
Knock an itty bitty woman hard to her knees.
It will make a small child cry as if its seen its mama for the last time.
I tell ya! Them four little letter called love can do some thangs.

Ghost Memory Quilt

The ghost of our past in our ears are like pathways of knowledge, wisdom and passion to seek out and empower us to pull up others by the boot straps and send them soaring up on high!
The adversity and stumbling blocks might make us fall down but we can always get back up and try again.
Our hurt and pain might blind us from seeing our positive outcome further down the road. Eventually the blur does fall away and the picture before us becomes clear.
Don't let the next trial keep you victimized. Break free of the chains that threaten to keep you shackled and tied down. Turn that ordeal of negativity into mad fuel to feed the fire that will be victorious over what ever was the source of your oppression.
Take flight on wings to see beyond the outer limits because your mind possess infinite possibility that knows no limits beyond your will to search past the next horizon.
Accept support system when you are weak, so you can stand strong united on the home front. This offer is only a hand up not a hand out for you to take baby steps until the ground is no longer shaky under your feet.
Pay attention while building your self back up in the presence of your enemy use any perceived weakness to your advantage to give the element of surprise. Never let your other hand know what the other can do, it may very well save your life.
Remember you are never alone because true friends never let you soar solo. They may not always be who you expected them to be but you will know them because the will urge you on and push you to go for the gold. Never forget your life history. Harness that memory. When the opportunity knocks even if you have to push a wedge in the door jam to make it happen. Never cease to pull someone else up out of the jaws of

there hell. Thus adding on to our ghost of memories quilts that help us keep the cycle of healing, renewal and the will to persevere against all odd alive. The true key to success is keeping faith in the hearts of the ones once in distress, the hope for ones still crossing that bridge, and the ones that perished to know there lives were not giving in vain. Gods blessings and love!

Chapter 2

Matters of the Heart
love romance and relationships

Wild Flower Tamed
Unbridled Love
My Love Oasis
Caught Out
Private Room
How Does It Feel?
A Moonlight's Dream
Battle Won
A Woman and a Man's Love
My Love for You
Professing Love to Late Saying Goodbye Too Soon
Fresh Start
If Only You Knew
It's a Sad-Sad Day to Be in Love
My One True Wish
The Right

Wild Flower Tamed

Be careful what you do to me.
I'm a flower blowing wild and free in the breeze.
Who needs to be rooted in the soil of your garden.
To be tended to with lots of love and care.
Water me with your soulful voice, so I may grow strong.
Assure me that I am protected.
Fertilize me so I may feel secure.
Knowing my place is by your side.
Pluck the weeds, prune me back.
Just enough for me to know I am my own flower.
Unique from your average garden variety.
Give me shade and sunlight when required.
My flowering will enhance our togetherness.
You will long to tend to your garden long after dark.
For I will bloom the prettiest blossoms, shining bright.
Yielding a most potent fragrance.
A scent that all your very own.
A smell of my wild love tamed just for you.

Unbridled Love

Love is so easy to get into but hard as hell to get out of.
You smile, they smile. You laugh, they laugh back.
Everything seems so right between you. You never want that feeling to end.
But, it does start to go wrong. Where, when and how you know not.
You stop talking, they start talking more. You stop listening, they get louder.
You start stepping back, they come closer. You leave, they follow.
Why can't it just be over? You say, they say. Why does it have to end?
You agree to try again, but your heart still feels like no ones home.
Your mind is closed down. Your body begins to be unresponsive.
Just going through the motions, the lack of emotion begins to take there toll.
Yet you smile at them while, your inner spirit screams out, no more its over!!!
They smile back at you, thinking everything's going to be alright, but you know better. As they come closer to you go rigid from this embrace you can no longer tolerate. You whisper to them as you push away, its over!!! No more smiles, no more laughs, no more embraces, no more wishful thinking it is over!!! Please don't talk, just listen. Please don't follow when I leave.
Just stay and move on. It will hurt a little but this is really for the best.
Love is supposed to be shared by two people. Not you, yourself and a figment of me. Please don't beg for it to be otherwise, just accept it. Wipe the tears from your eyes for I have none to shed over this departure. Except that it didn't happen sooner. Don't ask for explanation or place blame. Don't ask where did I go wrong or look for faults. Don't make promises or say what if I change? None of that matters because or minds are already made up, our hearts are already closed, our bodies have already gone cold. The judgment has already been passed. The sentence has been read, it over! Goodbye!

My Love Oasis

I want to float on a lily pad surrounded by tall grass and shoots in the middle of an oasis with waterfalls that sparkle like diamonds.
I'll be laying on my lily pad in the nude, resting my head in your lap. Your softly stroking my breast as soft purring escape my breath.
The stars come out to smile on our faces.
The grass waves softly in the wind.
The trees fold over to give us privacy. The animal dance a jungle beat to put is in the mood.
The tides provide a steady course on which way to go.
The water acts like a mirror and reflects our images of love back at us.
How are pad conforms to our every movement.
As we near the falls I achieve ecstasy.
As we go over the edge the thrill of falling as were wrapped tight inside of each other takes flight and soars.
My heart skips a beat as we near the bottom of the falls.
How the water foams up to greet us basking us in our own escalations. We hit bottom, my body burst into a thousand pieces and you swim for them like treasure in a chest where you put the pieces of my inner self back together again.
Take me to shore and breathe life back into me once again.
I breathe with the soft song of you on my lips, a smile on my face, love showing all over you I close my eyes, resting in your warm embrace blanket by my lily pad know I have found my love oasis.

Caught Out

You got me caught out on a string strumming a song for your love. Dancing a gig for your sexual healing.
Ready to drop on bended knees to pray and profess my sinful thought that lay in wait on my mind and come forth from my lips in sweet ecstasy.
I have to love, it may be wrong but I don't want to be right. So please steal a way for me to have just a moment of your time.
For it wont take me but a moment to seal this feeling with a kiss on your secret spot.
Just a moment to make my heart flip turning my frown into a smile. My body will quiver making you shake.
Come here and kiss me with a feeling.
Enter me with assurance only you can deliver, hearing the octaves going up and up in my call of passion.
My dance is tickling your every fantasy making me feel like sixteen burning sixteen candles as you turn my virtue into raw uninhibited fuel for your fire.
Keep stroking it. Make the blaze come alive getting better and better each time we are together.
Taking me faster and faster as if we were on a ride.
Then still your self for a while.
Listen to the purrs while you lay it on my spot.
Feel the explosion as the fire works go off on your soul.
Losing site of time and space. Catching my breath in mid stride.
Waiting to exhale with every bump and grind.
Call my name, scream it louder and louder baby.
Let me hear you feel it deep down in your manhood.
Let me see it in your face. Your eyes rolling back in your head, in the quiver of a smile on your lips.

The fanning of your hand for air. The curling of your toes. Your rocket is now cleared for take off. Your sail let out to float your boat. My kitty says that the cats meow. As you go snorkeling taste from my sea drink from my ocean, drift into sweet slumber worth a thousand dreamless nights.

Private Room

Come into my private room throughout the room. Lay on my bed an oasis of silk sheets and rose petals with pillows galore. Listen to my song, how it gets you in the mood. Watch the reflection of my dance all around you. Which one am I: the one down on my knees ready to take you all in. the one bent over from the back ready to beg you to take it some more. The one laying on my back spread eagle for you to drink your fill. Or last but not least, the one on top ready to ride out like a real soldier on his mount. You choose, for this night is all yours. What goes on in here stays in here. Come lay your head on my bosom and drink nectar from my flower. sting me like a honey bee. Send me buzzing on a natural high. Make me soak and wet so I may drench your body with my natural oils to massage your every nook and cranny. Making your every fiber standing on end. Feel the tingling sensation from your head to your toes. What was once cols now grows warm. What was once soft is now hard. What was once dry is now moist ready willing and able to handle your every move. You scream I scream louder baby for the walls of this room are only for my ears to hear. Tell me how you like it? Tell me who is the best? Say my name, now! and I will give you no mercy! I take no prisoners only willing participants. I'll set your mind free as I lick the juices from your sweet fruit. Wipe the sweat from your brow so you can see the glow radiating from my body as it give you sweet milk in response to all of the good planting and tending we've been engaging in down inside this private room where only you can enter.

How Does It Feel?

Here! Look into my face! What do you see? How does it make you feel? Here! Touch my blossoms! How do they feel? Here! Kiss on my neck, nibble on my back! How does it feel? Here! Rub on my spot! How does it feel? Here! Spank on my back side! How does it feel? Here! Now stick me with your member and stroke me till I cant take no more, then stop! Ask me here! How does it feel? I will tell you. It feels like the heavens and earth has come and pushed the rain away. Like birds have come to play my favorite song. The breeze blows just right to keep me cool. The desires of my mind have been set ablaze. The embers from the fire on my body have been stoked to burn at a steady pace evaporating into the air for you to breath in. In remembrance for another day when I am not near. Something passes you by an d you will say I know how that feels!

A Moonlight's Dream

I'm waiting, anticipating and expecting your arrival.
I'm dreaming of your entrance as the lights dim.
You glide over to me with your twinkle in your eye.
Your glimmer in your smile.
How glad it makes my heart.
Can you hear it beating?
Waiting to stop.
You reach down and kiss me with those sugary lips.
Can you sense the shiver in my bosom?
Your hand pushes my spine closer to you.
My breath catches in a waiting to exhale moment.
We're on stage, everyone wants to be me.
You lean me into your arms for a long embrace.
My legs start to give.
Just pull me in closer like a magician.
Captivating your audience with those tricks.
Making me want more and more.
But there's no hurry.
We have all night for this.
Your fingers sway playfully over my shoulders like a pianist.
Making my hair stand on end, like musical notes.
Only you can hear them.
Those vibration swaying in the wind.
Can you feel me floating on cloud nine.
You lay me back to glide your hands down my body.
The sheen you see on my face is getting heavy.
The low rumble in my throat turns to soft purring.
You fall gracefully on me.

Basking in my heat, cooling me slowly.
I passionately lose my essence.
With every concerning thrust of your vulnerability.
You place on my mind a photo.
Worth being a Kodak moment.
I lay wrapped in a midnight breeze.
From the lingering scent of your exit.
I wake long after your departure to a glowing sun rise.
I'm already wanting, waiting, and expecting your entrance once more.

Battle Won

CAN YOU HEAR MY CALL, ANSWER TO MY CRY.
GIVE ME MY WAR PAINT.
I AM ABOUT TO ENTER THE BATTLE FIELD OF LOVE.
MANY WILL ENTER IT. I
T WILL BE A HARD FIGHT FOR MY CONQUEST IS STRONG WILLED AND DOES NOT BEND EASILY TO JUST A GOURGEOUS BODY.
IT WILL TAKE ALL MY SKILLS AND KNOWLEDGE TO POSSES HIM FULLY.
OUR MEETING PLACES ARE INFINITE BECAUSE WE HAVE THE WHOLE WORLD IN WHICH TO ENCOUNTER EACH OTHER.
I MUST ALWAYS BE READY BECAUSE I'LL ONLY HAVE MY SENCES TO GUIDE ME AT THE RIGHT CHANCE MOMENT AND THEN AND ONLY THEN WILL I MOVE IN ON MY PREY AND OVER POWER HIM WITH MY MESMORIZING EYE AND STUNNING DANCE AND THEN ALONG EMBRACE TO CRUMBLE HIM TO HIS KNEES WHERE THEN AND ONLY THEN WILL I TASTE OF HIS FRUIT AND BRING FORTH HIS IRREPRESSIBLE DESIRE TO NO LONGER FIGHT ME, BUT BE MY CAPTIVE WILLING, MY LOVE SLAVE, BRANDED BY MY HAND.
STUNG BY MY TONGUE, LASHED BY MY BREAST. TIED BY MY LEGS AND TAMED BY MY HEART AND KNOWING I HAVE WON BY MY SOUL DESIRE TO CROWN YOU MY KING ON THE DAWNING OF A NEW DAY WE SHALL WALK OUR GROUNDS NOT IN BATTLE STANCE BUT AS MAN AND WOMAN ON A JOURNEY OF LOVE AND NEVER ENDING

DESIRE TO PLEASE AND POSSES ONE ANOTHER DEEP DOWN IN THE DELVES OF OUR INNER MOST BEING EACH OTHER.

A Woman and a Man's Love

A woman love is more precious than rubies for she gives you life when you lay upon her and you are happy as long as you are in her presence because she is tender and you are only beloved in her sight. She whispers words only for your ears to hear, only for your heart to bear witness too. She brings honor when you embrace her fully. The sky backs away and the clouds come to play, spilling forth there dew as she puts you to sleep all so sweetly. You wake with her thoughts wrap around your neck as fingers playfully sway ever so lightly in the balance as the words she spoke take on feet and begin to walk themselves on a table written down specifically for your heart. Is this woman not everything you desire? Does she not wear well as an ornament about your head? Gracefully skilled in all manners of love and passion this woman can bring your crown, glory worth the praises of millions, and artifact that is priceless only to the life she breathe into you. Keep her and your life shall be full.

A mans love is like a deep kiss on the lips, it taste better than fine wine. His fruit is sweet to the taste. His body is so that he can take your head in one hand and embrace your body fully with the other and his smell is like wild flowers tantalizing all your senses making you feel like a well of living water, dripping dew on his spring root that grows strong to deflower you down in the garden he takes you there—here he speaks cloyingly into your ear—this is where all my love comes from as he places his lips of honey and milk on yours as it flows under your tongue all is gone as if in deep sleep, but wait he speaks again and your heart wakes as if in answer to his movement as in voice his body tells you like a knock on a door open for me because my head is filled with wine and my body with hypnotic dance brought on by night fall. He tells you to put your hand by the hole in the door. Can you feel his stallion move for you? You spread yourself open for this mane and he slides over you with the scent of incense, his fingers exude oils for your every pleasure and as he takes you to every rooftop you know you are filled with the vine that has been tended for many ages because you are drunkenly mesmerized that even in sleep you speak of this man that stirs you up keeps you until you are pleased many waters can not quench this man love, nor can any flood drown him out of you for he has set himself like a stamp on a mailing to your heart, like a rancher brands his cattle, like marriage his love is till death do you part.

My Love for You

Time may come and time may go, but something that will never change is my love for you.
We may laugh and smile. We may yell and shout.
We may sway back and forth like a leaf in the wind.
Still my love for you will never change.
Through sad times, through rough patches, through times of uncertainty,
I'll be there because my love for you will never change.
Throw things that don't work and can't be fixed.
Through heart aches and heart breaks.
When the fire has fizzled and the physical has wasted away.
I'll stand by your side because my love for you will never change.

Professing Love to Late Saying Goodbye Too Soon

I call you but you do not answer. I see you but you act like I'm not their. I touch you but you act like you don't feel it. I tell you the truth but you don't believe me. What is wrong that was just right with you only a moment before? Can one instance change everything that we were harnessing? Why do you tell me you will come but don't show up. Why do you not call? Am I not pleasing to you anymore? Do I not have feeling too? Do you not think about my hurt and pain? Didn't I try to build you up? Make you feel more of a man. Didn't I prove myself over and over that I am the best you ever had. Yes, you say. So why would I do anything different to change those feelings and trust you have in me? What brain were you thinking with when you promised to keep me and spend eternity with? Is it the one on top of your head or the one betweens your legs that has you in a state of confusion about what's going on between us? You say you have doubts, but you will let me show you otherwise. Yet you still don't answer me, touch me, or see me fully. So again I ask you what is wrong? What have I done that you yourself have asked me to do? Did you not think it through? Were you afraid I could not pull it off? Maybe because if the tables were turned you would not be so strong, you would give in? well I am not you. I am strong. I have been through so much. And of all people I thought you would be able to see that. I thought you believed in me? Wanted to talk to me? Wanted to see me? Wanted to be touch by me? Wanted to know how to keep me? Maybe we were both wrong? I don't know but please tell me yes or no because I don't know how much more of cat and mouse I can play. When I've fallen so deep on the verge of being on the edge of being in love with you. But its not to late to go back and undo what has been done. Because its only been such a short while. But I must know one way or the other. I am on the rise to the very core of losing my mind. If we can't reach a solution to this situation we have develop. I might just die a hypothetical death. Never ending like one frame of a movie played over and over again. I leave you with this to ponder that one day you will know on your own that I was true and then you'll call me but I won't answer you. You will see me but I will not see you. You will touch me and I will not feel you. You will tell me the truth and I neither will believe you. I will come and not show. I will not tell you I will call and not do so. Unlike you I know how your hurt and pain feels. I will only promise that which I can keep. I think with my mind, my heart and my soul. The heat from betweens my legs says I should stay and fight. But the lord has told me to be a woman and move on. From this day forth I only have a reminder of you like the passing wind. Once in a while it blows a little briskly to let you know it can be there but most of the time you'd never know it was not. Goodbye.

Fresh Start

My relationship is on the fritz, it says the thrill is gone!
My man says he's having a Jones attack.
I've left him all alone and sad.
My heart is breaking like shatter glass.
Wont you please baby please come back home?
Give me just a little more of your sunshine please.
He begs and pleads to give him one more chance.
My eyes close on the window to his soul no longer feeling his vibe.
He continues to present his case.
I've turned a deaf ear to his run of the mill noise.
He signals me to come closer to him.
I continue to make stride in going a whole other direction.
I see the new horizon just over the next bend.
Just a few more steps to freedom, oh! How sweet it smells!
Not to sound mean because I do care for that old friend of mine.
I just don't need none of his bull any more.

If Only You Knew

I'm missing you, thinking of you.
Think how much I could love you.
I know you probably could care less 'cause you don't even know I exist.
If only you could see me.
I'd open a whole new plateau.
We could swim in the limelight and sway by the moonlight.
We could stay and play awhile.
Make a picture perfect moment ripple in time and feel the effects to last a life time.
If only you could feel me.
We could steal away for awhile and explore the joys of intimacy. Passion that burns late in the midnight hour sending smoke up the chimney stack.
Only if you could read my mind, you'd know how I desire you so.
How deeply in passing you touch my core.
How openly I want to taste of your essence.
Pluck your minds tender soul.
Lay it on my bosoms to listen to the strum of my ever beating heart.
If only I could be the one your heart desired I could tickle your fancy and make all your fantasy's come true.
If only I could take a chance and stop you in your tracks, then maybe you could know.

It's a Sad-Sad Day to be in Love

It's a sad-sad day to be in love.
It sneaks up on you in a blink of an eye. Blinds you in a flash.
It takes over your mind, body and soul.
Making you crumble to the floor, weak in the knees, bent over with a sour taste in your mouth.
It punks you into taking the big plunge only to land head first in the lake of cold water.
Love makes you into a fool, have you acting like a clown.
Making an a** out of yourself for those few ups and downs.
On a roller coaster that has you going around and around.
Cutting off your laughs in midair coming off a natural high.
Only to cry yourself a river, trying to figure out where you went wrong and why me?
Yes, it's a sad-sad day to be in love.
There are no winners to it.
Every ones a loser because it suckers you into falling for it, hard without a seatbelt, a parachute, a 50/50 chance, a life line, or someone to call for help. It gives you the Sunday Blues and the stormy Mondays and the Friday jitters when your all alone trying to search for the warm and security it promise to provide and failed to deliver its like having an emergency but not being able to reach 911 because your outside your coverage area and you can't hear me now because your closed minded to the idea that maybe love really doesn't live here anymore.
We don't want to look at ourselves and realize that our greatest fears have come true that we may just be unsuitable for some things so strong as love.

My One True Wish

If only I could get the inside of your eyes to see the inside of my minds eyes it would see love over flowing from a cup waiting for your lips to touch to warm you from the inside out. To shower you with kindness all day long. To provide you with sweet dream through out your nights rest. To be the one you communicate all your thoughts and concerns too. Want to be your life partner, the one you grow old with. I don't want to change who you are. I just want the chance to show you that not all people are the same. T wish you could see my heart. How it beats your name in your absence keeping my mind stead fast on you. I wish I could break the chains that hold you at bay from me. That keep you from fully opening yourself up to me. I wish I was your antidote that could cure your hurt and pain, so that you could fully trust me. I wish you had the same passion and faith in me as you have in our Lord and Savior. Then maybe you could Love me whole heartily. Loose the crutch and grab on to yourself worth, be proud of what you can do instead of what you can't. then and only then will your self esteem rise. You to will believe in the confidence I know you posses. Stop and smell the roses. Know that its alright to tell people no. believe me they will find another way. You'll feel better too, because you took out time for self for a change. If you don't take care of self first, you wont be around for the things you really do want and need to do. Stop and look in the mirror sometimes and be flattered at what you see. There is a beautiful person looking back at you, accept the fact that you are that person. Be honest to yourself first, admit that you want to make love everyday. Its okay to be scared about being able to perform or satisfy your mate. Realize it, accept it, then let it go! Because if it happens, it will happen. If you harp and worry about it you just prevented it from happening naturally. Relax and take a deep breath. Believe me when you ask about my feeling and I answer by telling you how I felt. Take note of this when in doubt young and old people everyday are intimate in some way or another. Only 35% of them are achieving one single climax the other 65% aren't having any at all.

You can take pride and scream it from the roof tops because we are both young and old and together we climax more in one session than a whole population of people having copulation on a daily basis. Hell we only do it on average 3 times a month. Know its hard for you to believe that I have closed the chapter on Jody, but I need you to know that even though we have a little life that bonds us together to care for, the personal life we once shared is over. It is closed. They always say never judge a book buy its cover. Well I read it, I lived it, and I can honestly say I should of took word of mouth and left it on the shelf. I hope that when your with me, me is really who you know you are with, who loves you and truly wants to be with you who trust in you as well as believes in you. I hope you see me as the odd ball out different from the crowd and that you are special enough to have the best. One day everything you have given to me I will return tenfold. I pray whatever comes our way good or bad we will continue to stick together. Through thick or thin always keep the lines of communication open so that our love for one another will continue to grow and prosper.

The Right

What gives you the right to stand up and demand my love? Who told you to open up a flood gate of emotions that I thought didn't exist anymore? Who told you to become the FBI and force me to testify my love for you, only to offer me no witness protection program. After I signed, sealed and delivered the verdict to you? Who told you I was the one to for fill all of your desires all for the price of admission. A few therapy session to make my heart all looped to loop. Going pitter patter for some feelings I haven't had in so long. Who lead you to believe that I even remotely want to live in the thrill of the chase of your lusty hunt for my essence? Who asked you to become the superhero and complete a mission impossible to free me from the I-robot I had become. So accepting to be who followed the three laws that kept me safe. Bound to a eight by ten space which was my personal dwelling place. My place was supposed to be impenetrable from your love. Who asked you to do all these things to weaken my defenses to take me off my guard. Tell me who asked you to show me how to do this thing called love and once I stood up on it and built my rock on it? Who gave you the freaking right to try and erase it and make it like it never even happen? How dare you tell me I'm not worthy just because you find out my love you started was not the love you thought you wanted to have. What am I supposed to do with it now that you have no use for it. I just can't turn it off, I can't stop hearing it, feeling it and seeing it. It has overpowered me with your smooth smile. Your silk touch, your swagger lines that flow so easily from those sinuous lips and beaming eyes. So tell me Mr. I'm so good! Who gave you the right to take my love like a thief in the night only to turn around in the light and pawn it like a bad habit for a twenty dollar fix?

Chapter 3

Mother and Child
a family too

Dear Child of Mine
A Mother's Love
Ode to My Mother
Cross, Candles and 2 Rings for My Mother
Just Me and You
Here's
A Family
A Marriage Vow
Sunshine Man, Moonlight Darling

Dear Child of Mine

Precious child.
Child only beloved by one.
Always cherished and spoiled by your mothers hand.
Only as the one who labored to bring you into this world can. I pour out my soul to you. I love you and miss you so.
Mere words alone could not express the missing I go through with you not being here.
Its like receiving a knock at the door, when open your not there.
My heart aches and reminisces about when you were little.
You used to place your small hand in mine and look up with those big brown eyes. You'd smile up at me and I'd give you a great big hug to hide my tears of joy. As the years past you grew to place a many memory on my mind.
and even though that hand grew to be my size you never stopped being that little child of mine.
When someone laughs and it reminds me of you I start turning back the hands of time to way back then.
When some one resembles you passes my way I shed a tear because I want to reach out to that dear child of mine and hold that small hand in mine.

A Mother's Love

A mother's love for a child begins right at conception even before we know you are a boy or girl. Just the mere fact that you are growing inside us makes us love you. Upon your arrival we go through near death to birth you in the world. I know no greater love than that. After we take you home you are so fragile, so delicate a small copy of us and what's to come. A mother must care for your every need. In response you greet us with your smiles, your cooing, your out stretched hands reaching for ours. I give you mines and your fingers latch on tight. Absorbing the security and protection of a mother's love. When your in a room alone, fussing, and crying. You quiet just from the entrance of your mothers smell. When you hear her voice you will smile. Upon seeing her face you will laugh for joy. When something wrong, your frighten or sick their nothing like a mothers touch to soothe you like a sweet lullaby, sending you off to dream land. I know no greater love than that. When you begin to walk and talk and imitate us we are so proud and dismayed at times. And when you fall and get a boo-boo, nothing is more calming than a mothers hug and kiss. It lets you know better than any medicine that every thing is alright. Who is the last to see you off on your first day of school and the first face you seek when it is out? Your mothers smiling face who missed you twice as much as you did. I know no greater love than that. When your older and are afraid of the bogeyman, who comes and tucks you in and whispers a prayer for your sweet slumber. When loves first crush crushes you. Who tells you they weren't worth it and you'll find a better love next time? Then give you lots of tissue and cries all night long with you. And when you go away to find your own way, who keeps your room just the way it was when you last were there. When you have your first child who's love comes back to you in a blink of an eye.? Your mother's love. There none greater than that.

Ode to My Mother

A Mother is the heart and amour to her child.
She dies in birth to give her child life.
She lights a path in which her child can follow so it wont get lost.
She surrounds you with love and joy so the child can be safe and secured.
She teaches the child right from wrong.
Steers you in the way of the Lord so you may have everlasting life.
She knows from the time she bore you, you begin to die.
A mother knows your time with her is only for a little while.
She prays for you to be blessed from day one.
A mother is not only your friend she is your angel in disguise.
She knows how to give just the right hug and kiss to heal all your wounds.
The right words to soothe your hurt feelings.
She is like chicken soup to your spirit good to the very last drop.
She is the very foundation for self awareness, self esteem, self empowerment so you can be strong.
She is the right hand side of you until you are grown.
But, remember to your mother you are always her baby.
You know the saying, daddy's maybe mommies always!
Ode to my mother, as you celebrate your birthday I want to thank God for creating you, just so you could give life to me.

Cross, Candles and 2 Rings for My Mother

I have this picture of a cross, candles and 2 rings in my heart for 3 reasons: the cross because from the time I could remember you always said, Lord, Jesus Christ, have mercy. That let me know there is a God and you wanted him to be there for me night and day and to believe him and rely on him for the things know and unknown. I know it wasn't always easy with me but you never stopped calling on him for my behalf even when things were not always right. The candles represent a guide of light in which to find my way back home into your heart and know everlasting love only the way a God trusting fearing mother could give. I love you, You are my Mother always and forever!!!!!!! Last but not least the intertwined rings for the times we had to go round and round for me to get that Love sometimes hurts and it will bring you through a better person. Sometimes as a parent you have to be rough because the world can be cruel those rings let me know that even when absent we are together and though even grown we never cease to learn from one another, never stop loving each other, never stop being a help to each other because we are always encircling one another. Love you always, Your Daughter!

Just Me and You

Just me and you laughing & talking
Just me and you kissing and hugging
Just me and you real loving all day long
Just me and you we don't need no one else
Just me and you we don't have to worry about a dam thing
Just me and you side by side we have each others back
Just me and you making each others wishes come true
Just me and you keeping it real down to earth
Just me and you up till the sun rises just being lovers and friends
Just me and you being strong for each other
Just me and you blending 2 hearts, can you feel them beating as 1?
Just me and you being 2gether again has us caught up like the first time
Just me and you losing control turning each other out
Just me and you forever just loving us

Here's

Here's to us meeting and falling in love at first sight.
Here's to us and loves first kiss.
Here's to us and loves first embrace.
Here's to us and loves first union.
Here's to us and loves first engagement.
Here's to us and loves first courtship.
Here's to us and loves first wedding.
Here's to us and loves first family.
Here's to us and loves first anniversary.
Here's to us and loves happily ever after.
Here's to us and loves first toast of wishful things to become a first for us!

A Family

A family can be any group of two or more people.
That come together and loves, shares and cares for each other.
A family provides all of your basic needs and a few of your wants.
A family provides a shield of protection from danger.
A family raises you with the right values and helps you plant the seed to branch out on your own.
A family is strong for all parties, even for the one weakling.
A family doesn't uphold you when your wrong but they don't throw you out to the wolves when your already down and out.
A family should love you unconditionally even if its fed to you from a long handle spoon.
A family always leave room for change.
Even if its difficult to carry out at times.
A family doesn't just cease to exist because of ones passing on because the others are always left with your memories to carry them on.
And most importantly a family that prays together stays together.

A Marriage Vow

Marriage is a union that is pleasing unto God.
It brings one man and one woman together into one being that functions as one mind, body and soul.
It becomes sacred and should be cared and tended properly so love can grow and prosper abundantly. Be fruitful and multiple.
As your wife I want you to know that I will be there at ever curve in the bend to love you and care for you. That when your up on mount high I'll be there to enjoy the ride.
When you are down low hitting rock bottom fast, I'll already be there waiting for you to plant a kiss and turn that sadness into a smile.
When in good health I'll waste it not.
If you get ill I'll hold you close to give you comfort to get well. And if danger comes your way I'll give myself to keep you safe. I'll do all of this for nothing in return but for your love.
As you husband I want you to know that I'll love you till the end of time. I will labor long and hard to bear good fruit for you, never causing you shame or despair. I will make a place for you to set a watch on my heart to continuously keep count of our long life together.
I promise to listen and hear when we are communicating.
To be open and honest because even the truth hurts some times.
I promise you passion as long as were both able. I will shield and protect you from harm. You will have no worries in these arms. And long after were gray and old I'll still be in love with you, too!

Chapter 4

Deliverance
Christianity, inspirational, prayer

Sinners' Prayer
This Is a Battle
I'm Thanking the Lord for You Today
Call on Him
Deliverance
Loss of One's Child
Foundation
Accept Him
Lift Me Up
Dwelling Place
Satan Deceit, God Rescue
He Thought of Us First
Wake Up

Sinner Prayer

I thank the lord for me for I am a sinner with a prayer, that screamed out for help. I could have been just another lost soul, all broken and battered. But the Lord felt mercy and he gave me grace. He administered to my spirit like a good doctor tends to bad wounds. He sent a Shepard to show me the way. He left all sorts of signs and miracles so I would not get lost on the short and narrow path. And when I slipped and fell he was there to catch me. He carried me till I could stand on my own 2feet again. The Lord did all this for me, not because I'm perfect. Remember I am that sinners prayer.

My mind became like mush and I could not put 2and 2 together, I felt that I was being snuffed out, left out to sea to drown in my own sorrows. I felt that I was not worthy to live; I had almost given up all hope. Then like the clearing in the deep blue sea he was there with a life raft for me to grab onto. He said I made you in my image, I will never let you perish. I loved you so I gave my only begotten son, so that you—and I do me you with your sinners prayer could even obtain everlasting life. I thought with a sad look on my face; I've done so much wrong; I've caused so much hurt. I've been wrong and I've been hurt. I had a confused look on my face.

He said repent child, correct your ways. I start to cry, he said dry your eyes girl and pray a righteous prayer! I start to tremble and shake.

The Lord says, Listen, Hear, and Obey my Word!

I straighten up, dried my eyes, and with a smile I grab on to his life raft whole heartily.

He said, Now Live with Courage, Strength and Blind Faith in Me!

I thank him for me because of his word I no longer live in a shroud of doubt, fear or dread because he does even answer me; a sinner prayer.

This Is a Battle

This is a battle, put on your war paint and shout out your war cry for the Lord. This is spiritual warfare that that you cannot escape from. You either live for everlasting life with the father or you burn in eternal damnation with the serpent.

Shepard's gather your flock, let them not stray away. Prayer, pray feverishly on bended knee for our salvation. Choirs sing out a joyful noise for Jesus. He is coming again for his people and this place will be no more. Christians, all believers of the one true God call on some one today unsaved, of little faith, or just plain ignorant of his existence. Witness to them for our savior for that's one more soul entering into the holy of most holy places.

This battle will be fierce you must arm yourself well for there will be many that will come in his name to trick and persecute you. You will have to be watchful, put on your full armor of the Lord. Listen to your spirit it will never lead you astray. Keep his words written on a secret tablet in your heart for there may come a time when his written word may be burned, but it can never be removed from your spirit. Keep a righteous walk about yourself and never think the grass is greener on the other side for the meek shall inherit the land and the unjust with all there glitz and glam shall be no more. Keep a pray on your lips and be faithful even when things look bleak. Lean not unto your own understanding his way may not be your way. Remember it is his will that must be done.

At the end of this battle let out a gleeful noise for there are many mansions in our fathers house. There are no worries their, there are no sad days, but there is joy and happiness, song of exhorting, and praising and worship going on there forever and ever.

I'm Thanking the Lord for You Today

I'm thanking the Lord for you today.
For that warm smile, that twinkles in your eye.
Yes. I thank him whole heartily for you today
Because of your kind words, that caring hug.
For being by my side, bringing flowers, and sending inspiring card to wish
me well.
I'm so glad the lord has you to do his work.
The calling to check that I'm fine, the coming by to see if I had a need.
I thank him for you and I'm so glad that he shines so brightly in
You.

Call on Him

Call on him, remember he is your Shepard, and seek him first because he is the light whom you shall fear. Knock and the door shall be open unto you. Don't be afraid to take a step because the lord will take 2 bountiful steps for you and when you can walk no more he will carry you.
Trust in him w/ all thy heart and he will never forsake you. Lean not toward your own understandings because Gods knowledge is not our own, your plan may not be his plan. Be patient and wait on him.
And always remember the faith of a mustard seed can move mountains.

Deliverance

I'm trapped inside of a trap with no way out. I'm physically bound to my trap. My mind grows weary from my confines. It just me, myself and I in this dark place not being able to see or feel. Oh, this trap is suffocating, only if I knew the magic word like abracadabra to make it all go away, but I can't instead when ever I move it moves in closer. When I think it gets darker. Oh where is the light the one side I can walk out of I know it's there. Where is your knight in shining amour when you need a damsel in distress to be rescued? The one moment when the light goes off in your head, you say eureka I've got it! My heart has even stilled it self as if no hope of being free to breath again, how it loves to exhale, but that what has me trap in the first place. Love, it's blinded me. It's bounded me, its got hold of me physically and mentally. I can't move or think without it up and getting stronger on me. Causing me to get weaker with every growing need. It feeds on me getting better as I draw closer to my resting place. It is shedding me taking on new life. Giving birth to a new identity that is a bustle of joy to be here. preparing to live a long and vicarious life, me in my trap is only a small grain of salt in this new life the sky soars with clouds everywhere as I walk to my final destination a voice whispers that its okay to be scared but once you pass my gates all your chains shall fall away and your mind will be free and you shall see true paradise because I will rain down praise and shower you with my eternal life and you shall be loved unconditionally and unyielding because you are my child. You are a child of GOD, where his love is everlasting and given freely. At last I am where I belong wrapped in his Love and Grace. Jesus meets me with open arms and I look through the clouds one final time, I know I have been rescued from internal damnation and I take on wings to cross over into my little bit of Heaven. How everything glows and shouts out a joyful noise. I shine bright as a shooting star in the dark night I am free as a lamb covered in the blood of Jesus, at last I have been delivered! Amen!

Loss of One's Child

Something happen today that a parent should never have to experience, that is the lost of ones child. I can only say I am sorry you had to lose yours because I don't know what it is like and do not care to try and imagine life with out mine. My heart goes out to you in your time of grief. And you have my deepest sympathy at this time and I wish and pray your grief will be short lived.

For God so loved the world he gave his only begotten son so if know one else knows he does. So call on him when you get down, he will lift you up. When all have left you to dwell alone, seek him, he will provide you comfort and companionship, and rest assured knowing that he will do what you could not and that is give your child everlasting life by his side for surely your child is in a better place now. With him there is no pain and suffering there is only joy and happiness all the day long.

So don't be sad or mad because God knows all you have been through and all you have done to make things right for he says he will put no more on us than we can bear.

He knows you have been strong and labored long and hard for the fight for your child. Now he said it was time for him to bear that weight for you to live to battle another day. For remember the war is just beginning and he needs all of his troops to be ready for another day.

We all take care of our own when they are not at there best, but God restores us and makes us brand new.

Bringing us into the light which is through his son Jesus Christ come love and blessings and eternal life.

Foundation

You are a rock, a stronghold, a solid foundation on which your house is built on.
If you get weak or crumble you must not give in.
put out more no matter how futile it may seem.
You must have feverish faith and God's strong will to lead you.
He will guide you properly in repairing all that has went wrong.
In good measures all that has been broken can be mended.
Once again you will become that rock, that stronghold, that solid foundation that has been reinforced.
Made new by God's good grace.
Believe and you shall see and feel it made so.
When you have said all you can say.
They have done all they can do.
Remember that it is all right because God always has the last say in the matter. Amen!

Accept Him

Today I long to walk with my mother and father, but I could not.
Why, you ask could I not? I couldn't because they both past away.
I am sad at my loss. Joyous at knowing they are in a better place.
I sit here thinking about who I would now cling too.
Who will nurture me, guide me? I hear a voice say you are not alone. I will be your mother and your father now. I have doubts.
The voice says fear not come and walk with me.
Tell me what ales you? What worries you?
Tell me about all your needs and wants.
What makes you happy or sad? Let me wrap you in my shield and protect you.
Let me shower you with good grace, love and blessings.
In return I ask that you acknowledge me as your God.
Know that when all else is gone I am always their.
If only you'll just let me in.
Wont you please accept me in your life today?

Lift Me Up

Lord, lift me up when I am down.
Place courage where there is fear.
Give strength where there is weakness so it may mate and give birth to strong will.
Reinforce my faith, Lord so it may not dally.
Pick me up and carry me back to the righteous path.
Lord please turn not away from me when I have sinned yet again. Humble me to fall on my knees to beg your forgiveness and mercy. Remind me that I am worthy in you.
Set ablaze those that seek to hurt me, lord let them know I am your child, too.
Take up your shield and place me under you're your wing.
Let my enemies not see me when they pass my way Lord.
Lord hear my cries deep in the night when all else is sleep.
Lord heal my burning flesh, soothe my aching bones, relax my weary mind, console and comfort my confused spirit.
Walk with me awhile. Down to the river Lord we go to cleanse me and wash me new.
Make me shine of rebirth, renewed and made over in your light.
Lord forgive the world and watch over my friends for they need you too.
I write this prayer in your son Jesus Christ's name, Amen!

Dwelling Place

I felt so all alone.
I made a few calls to talk to you, I got know answer.
I made a few visits, know was home. I went to all of our usual meeting places, you were not there.
I became dazed and confused.
Everything turned black.
I woke to the sounds of harps, the warmth of basking light on my forehead.
The cooling of a breeze across my body.
A soft but powerful voice spoke.
Why do you look for me so furiously?
do you not know me when you are standing right in front of me?
Do you not feel me when I am carry you?
When you are weak do you not know where I am housed at all times for you? I looked but at first I was blinded.
I felt the warmth spread over me.
My heart began to beat faster.
My eyes became clear.
I saw you just for a moment. A figment on my mind.
I knew you were real. I knew you still loved me.
I knew where you were. Inside my heart growing and strengthen me in my darkest hour.
I had let ill will move in, but at my breaking point you came and fought for me.
You gave my body healing. My mind rest. You renewed my spirit.
For that I am grateful. Eternally bound to you.
You are my lord and savior. Amen!

Satan Deceit, God Rescue

I feel I am nothing, a grain of salt is more something than me right now. I feel I am ugly, a flower has more beauty than I'll ever possess. My soul is tormented, will it ever find rest? My mouth has done nothing but profess truth, yet when the words fall upon open ears they claim they hear only lies. Why am I being hurt so? Can't you see my shatter heart? Does it not bleed enough for you to want to heal my wounds? Why do you cut deeper and compound my pain? Packing it down with vinegar so that it fester and grows worse still. Why can't you see me for me? Why must you always try and change me? What is defective on me so much that you continue to put me back on the return to makers bend? Do you not need love too. So why do you constantly keep playing dodge ball with giving love to me? Do I judge you? No! but you want to taunt and persecute me all of the time. Why must I be the one to yield? You are the one doing the crime. Yet I always seem to be doing the time. What do you want from me? When you give nothing of yourself to me. All I want is love, but all you give me is hate! Satan be still, know you have no dominion over me no more. Your life is full of deception and deceit. You live the life of a lie like a thief in the night. You rob steal and kill for your own self satisfaction. But low and behold your day is coming. Your time will end. I will be free from you. I will rise like butterflies high up in the sky. I will flutter from flower to flower with out a care in the world. I will abide and blend in to escape your torment, fate will intervene and rescue me from being prey to your dire travesty. He will give me refugee and leave you wondering that even though you were a great fear to me, making me appear to be small and fragile, with the Lord he makes me new and gives me strength and beautification. And even when you think you have closed me in, God say even then I can rest alone in him.

He Thought of Us First

Today may not have been as good as the last day and you might have to dig deep in the trenches to work on your well being.
After all we have to feed our bodies food and water to strengthen it.
We go to school to teach our minds. But most importantly we need to walk and talk with the Lord to save our souls.
Rejoice with him for being in your life and never look back on what was before.
Enter into the battle field with him by your side.
He will be your shield when times get rough. You are not alone.
When it is smooth sailing, forget not, the Lord is still there embracing you with his love and mercy.
You couldn't ask for any greater love than what he provides.
I'm so glad he thought enough to think of us first.

Wake Up

Wake up can you feel the warm glow, feel the cool breeze, hear the sweet song.
Give thanks for the Lord has made it so.
So get up, show some love for our heavenly father.
Give him all the praise and honor.
He gave you kindness and mercy.
He gave you everlasting life not because he had to but because he wanted too.
Shout out a joyful noise because good or bad he never leaves you.
He becomes your shield and comforter.
To sooth and protect your body and soul.
Fall down on your knees and pray to him in your secret place so that he may reward you for all your works openly and excitedly.
Most of all pass on the good news to another with good tidings, love in your heart and comfort in your arms.

Printed in the United States
66404LVS00013B/103-108